USSR TO UK

1941-1947

Lydia's Story

Written by Nicky Brown with Lydia Emmanuel

From USSR to UK

This is the story of the wartime experiences of an Armenian girl who was sixteen years old at the time of the German invasion and occupation of her country in 1941.   For two years she knew life under German rule in Crimea before being transported, with her mother, to Ludvigshaven in Germany as an East Worker.   There she worked in a hospital until the end of the war when, together with countless other refugees, she walked for ten days, arriving at Schlachters where she obtained work.   When UNRRA centres were established it was not long before she found work in their shop and eventually had the opportunity to work in UK as a displaced person.   Her story is told simply and without a great deal of emotion.   In her own words, **"What else could we do? We just had to survive."**

USSR TO UK

1941-1947

By
Written by Nicky Brown
With Lydia Emmanuel
©2005

ISBN 1-905023-01-4

FOREWORD

When I first offered to write Lydia's story she was hesitant and protested that it would not be of interest to anyone as so many thousands of people had similar stories to tell. By the time she was persuaded that the 'thousands of others' had probably not recorded their memories and that it was important for people, and her own family in particular, to learn of the times through which she had lived and survived, she was already nearly eighty years of age and had been a British citizen for more than fifty years. The war years had altered the course of her life, as it did for millions of others, but each individual story is different and eventually we started to piece together her account of those years and her subsequent arrival in England

Lydia's memory of so many of the events related here are as crisp and clear as if they were recent happenings. There are, of course, gaps but she has tried to recall little incidents which help to bring the past alive. First there was the arrival of the enemy and the occupation of her homeland by Nazi Germans. Later there was the long, frightening journey to Germany, accompanied by soldiers who dictated every movement of the transportees. In Ludwigshafen there were repetitive, dull, routine days with nothing more exciting or memorable happening than a visit to the pictures. There was homesickness but there was also companionship and shared confidences, laughter, tears, anxieties, fears and reminiscences. There were also the dreadful bombing raids over the twin towns of Ludwigshafen and Mannheim; the shortages, discomforts and all the frightful effects of war. Wartime life in Germany would appear to have been much like wartime life in England but with greater deprivation and fewer rations for the East Workers and prisoners. Summers were warm; winters were cold. Fuel in Germany was in short supply as it was in this country. The hospital where Lydia worked would have been kept as warm as possible but sixty years ago in wartime Germany this would not have afforded the patients much comfort. Later, as a refugee, Lydia knew what it was to be homeless and hungry.

Freedom brought new problems and anxieties. Although she relates various incidents in a matter of fact manner and can laugh now about the skirmishes with authority, she makes it clear that fraternising, looting and such activities were a matter of expediency if she and her mother were to survive. Now, in the twenty first century, young people will perhaps find it difficult to relate to those young people of whose wartime experiences they hear and read. They can have little understanding of the deprivations and hardships they endured. They had no choices. They had no freedom. They could not complain. And after the war when they thought they would be free, they knew a different kind of fear whilst they remained refugees in a defeated Germany. It was not until they experienced the true freedom of living in a democratic country with laws that protected its citizens that they could appreciate a just system of law and order.

Unhappily, at the present time, we have such wide freedom of choice and action, an almost complete lack of social taboos, and poor law enforcement that we are in danger of creating a new kind of fear: fear of once again allowing the bullies and those who clamour for more and more 'freedom' to do exactly as they wish, without a thought for the comfort of others, to dominate our lives and rob us of all that we fought for, honesty, justice, decency and security. Laws are for the comfort of everybody and need to be upheld - without exception, without complaint and without looking for scapegoats. Until it is accepted that we are all responsible for our own actions and end the present culture of blame and compensation, we will remain on the brink of anarchy and what kind of freedom is that?

I have tried to record Lydia's story as faithfully as possible. The historical details have been checked and are accurate; I have been able to research and verify facts on the Internet and discover other stories that confirm certain other events Lydia mentions. Whenever I have asked if she has regrets about not having achieved her earlier life's ambition, she shrugs her shoulders and simply says, 'There was a war.... It was the same for everybody. In the end I was lucky; I survived; I came to England, I had my nursing career, a good loving husband and a lovely daughter'. Perhaps she calls it luck; I call it pluck! It is said that adversity brings out the best or the worst in us. Lydia met all the challenges and I have been privileged to write this story, with her help, of a truly remarkable lady.

Note
Lida Karaeva was born in Simferopol on 5th January 1925. In Germany she was known as Lidia Karajan and when she arrived in England she made no objection to being called Lydia, the Anglicised version of her name. A further name change came when she married Dennis Emmanuel in 1953.
Nicky Brown.

Chronological Order of Events

1941

22nd June   4 am The advancing German Army crossed the Russian border.

11 am Vyacheslav Molotov announced state of war. Martial Law declared

3rd July   Stalin's first wartime speech

October   Fall of Sinferopol

Sebastopol under siege for next 250 days

December   Lydia started work in the local hospital where German Wounded were nursed

1942

June   Attempted evacuation of Sebastopol

July   Sebastopol fell to the Germans. Manstein's 11th Army Victorious

1943

January   Lydia's 18th birthday

July 5th   Operation Citadel

July 20th   Lydia and her mother left Simferol for Germany

Via Dnepropetrovsk to Poland via Lvov, then Przemysl, Krakcow, Breslau, Dresden, Leipzig, Frankfurt and Ludwigshafen

September   Devastating air raids on Ludvigshaven and Mannheim

1944

January	Beginning of health problems, typhus.
April	Returned to work after three months of illness.
September	General Vlasov given official authorisation to form his own Russian Liberation Army.
December	The end in sight. A cheerful New Year's Celebration.

1945

May	The end of the war and the beginning of Refugee Status
July	Lydia and her mother walked to Lindau am Bodensee approximately 125 Km. Where General Lampe was issuing certificates to refugees to give them an Identity. Walked another 10 Km. To Schlachters Worked on a farm, apple picking.

1945/46

Winter/Spring	UNRRA set up an office in Lindau Lydia was given work in the centre until move to England

1947

September	Lindau to Northern Germany and on to Hook of Holland Arrived in the UK

Acknowledgement

Many thanks to Lance Housley of Barnstaple Library for his kind help with producing the 1920's map.

The Beginning

Exams were over, the school term had ended and I was enjoying the luxury of lying in bed long past the usual time when loud, urgent knocking at the door awakened me. I struggled out of bed to find my school friend, Adele, somewhat agitated as she urged, "For goodness sake, get up and get dressed, Lydia. We have to go to school to hear what news our headmistress has to tell us". It was 22nd June 1941. I was quite perplexed and not so pleased to have to leave my bed but Adele was insistent that she had received a message, which she was to pass on, that all Komsomol members should report to the headmistress at once. She urged me to be quick and we arrived at the school breathless, anxious to hear what important announcement was to be made. Whilst we listened the atmosphere was tense. "Girls I have called you together to remind you and to warn you that we are living in anxious times. It is imperative that you should be on your guard, that you should be constantly vigilant....." We listened, bewildered, not fully understanding as she continued with her strong, yet vague, warnings and wondered why she had felt it necessary to call us back from our holiday to talk to us this way. What was she holding back? What was the meaning of it all? I had been dragged from my bed to be warned - of what? All we knew was that we were to be on our guard, be vigilant and wait for news. "What was all that about?" we asked each other, as we left the school, irritated by this anti-climax after having been called in for what we were told would be an important announcement.

Adele and I made our way towards the Square where we were surprised to hear from loudspeakers, mounted on posts, that Molotov, the Minister for Foreign Affairs, would be making an announcement at 11am which would be broadcast on loudspeakers (as not everyone had a radio). So what was it! We realised it must be something very serious as a sombre crowd began to gather to hear Vyacheslav Molotov, Assistant Chairman of the Council of the People's Commissars of USSR and the People's Commissars for Foreign Affairs, stammer his way through the announcement that the German air force had bombed five Russian cities, from the North to the South, at 4 am that morning and that the German army had crossed the Russian border and was advancing. Germany had declared war on the USSR. We couldn't believe it. It was impossible! My mind blank. Stalin and Hitler had already signed a pact, which we had felt had exempted us from the troubles of the west. Now we were at war with Germany. What could this mean to me a sixteen year old girl, living with a widowed mother in Simferopol. How would the war affect us? The simple fact, "We are at war with Germany...." could mean nothing at present except fill me with apprehension and curiosity. I could not feel fear because I knew nothing of what might lie ahead. With my headmistress's words about being vigilant still ringing in my ears I went home - and we waited.

We did not have to wait long for the effects of war to be visible. The speed with which the war machine was started up was quite astonishing. Martial law was declared on that very same day but already volunteers had stared to say their goodbyes to the tearful families who had come out into the streets to see them off. A labour conscription law compelled all men between the ages of 18 and 45 and all women between 18 and 40 to work eight hours a day constructing rudimentary defences to impede the progress of the advancing German army. War had come as a complete shock to Stalin at a time when the country was entirely unprepared but he appealed to the Soviet people for patriotism; his call for a popular militia - Narod-neoeopolchenie - was answered overwhelmingly.

My mother and I joined the group of volunteers who dug trenches around the city, fifteen to twenty of us in a group. This was hard, tiring work but we felt that we were helping to keep the enemy out. We worked during the summer evenings until the light faded each day. We worked and dug until we were exhausted. Street wardens were appointed to keep guard and to watch out for strangers. Changes came about quickly and with them came an air of suspicion and fear, many people becoming obsessed with the notion that spies were everywhere. There was one occasion when my Uncle Vanya, who was a store-man at the medical equipment department at the hospital, was returning home from work when some women began to call out 'Spy! Stranger! Arrest him!' Fortunately for my uncle, one of the medical students who happened to be passing, recognised him and shouted to these people, ' You stupid people. Can't you see it's only Uncle Ivan?' Otherwise I don't know what they might have done to him.

For the next few weeks we worked and we waited. We had a radio on which we could receive only one station and that was simply news from Moscow. We knew that the Germans were advancing but couldn't estimate how long it would be before they reached us in Simferopol, nor could we imagine what life would be like when they arrived, as we feared they would. As a sixteen year old I was simply curious and vaguely excited by the prospect of these changes, not knowing what lay ahead.

The German Army Arrives

In September school reopened but in different premises, the school buildings having been taken over as barracks for the newly enlisted soldiers to receive their basic training. The newspaper reports of terrible German atrocities were so frightful that my mother decided that we should go to stay with my uncle and aunt on the outskirts or the city where we hoped it would be safer. There we were on higher ground than the city and had good views uninterrupted by buildings as most of the dwellings in that area were bungalows. One evening, toward the end of September, my uncle said we should go with him and take a look at the fires burning in the centre of the town. The Germans had arrived and the destruction of the city had begun. Looting had started, even on the outskirts where we were. Shops and their meagre contents were abandoned leaving them wide open for the looters whose attitude was, 'If we don't take these things for ourselves, the Germans will take them or destroy them anyway'. Our only opportunity to join the looters came when we were passing a shop, which had been ransacked, with only tomato ketchup left. We hurriedly took several bottles of ketchup, as many as we could carry, our one and only expedition as looters! No doubt we would have used further opportunities had they occurred.

We could hear the Stukkas, the bombs and the gunfire which were aimed at the Russian army, but not the civilians. Toward the middle of October when we knew that Simferopol had fallen we made our way, cautiously, back home where we were met with scenes of such sadness and horror that I can picture them to this day: dead bodies of people and horses, wrecked buildings, crying women. There was a torso of a woman lying on the ground, broken bodies, and destruction everywhere. I felt numb, curious, bewildered by these horrific scenes. Some people told me that the Germans had hanged some Jews and Communists and they were left hanging from telegraph poles in the centre of the city. Amidst this devastation our home was all right and we were pleased to move back in.

The Beginning of a New Era

The standard of living in Stalin's Communist Russia at the time of my birth in 1925 was poor but because everybody, except the ruling classes, was poor we did not feel entirely deprived and life for my mother, my father, who was a doctor, and for me seemed to be happy. When I was only five years old my father died and that is when the course of our lives was altered. My mother had to go back to her work as a laboratory assistant in order to keep us both. Later, she resumed her studies to become a chemist and a teacher.

My childhood memories were happy although we had very little money. After kindergarten I started school at the age of seven, learning the usual subjects. At high school I learned German and the Roman alphabet. It was observed that I had a natural aptitude for languages and I always enjoyed learning new ones; this had stood me in good stead during my lifetime. Schooldays were fairly uneventful until storm clouds began to gather over Western Europe but we were not really too interested until 22nd June 1941 when Hitler actually invaded Russia.

Stalin made his first wartime speech on 3rd July when he appealed for sacrifices, patriotism and unity and decreed that in the occupied regions all valuable property should be destroyed, the scorched earth policy implemented and conditions made unbearable for the enemy.

The Germans arrived in Simferopol on 2nd October 1941. We then had German neighbours, German administrators and German soldiers living amongst us. By May 1942 the whole Crimea had fallen to the Germans except for Sebastapol which had been under siege from October 1941 and remained so for 250 days. An attempt to evacuate Sebastapol's populace was started in June 1942 but the city fell to the Germans in July. For us the war was already over. Manstein's 11th Army having been victorious, the Germans were now in charge and we had to learn to live with them. What else could we do when one's country was occupied? Food, of course, was very scarce and our only possibility was to barter whenever we had the opportunity to do so.

Before the Germans arrived my mother had been employed as a chemist in a factory where they extracted starch from flour for household and domestic use. After the starch had been extracted the remaining swill was used to feed the pigs. Mother bought a piglet which she left with a countrywoman to whom she gave two buckets of swill each day, one for our pig and one(in payment for looking after our pig) for hers. As soon as possible after the arrival of the Germans it was necessary to kill the pigs to ensure that they would be for our own consumption and not that of the enemy! I don't remember what became of the meat, as we had no means of preserving it. It was probably bartered for other things we needed to supplement our 100 grams of black bread. Flour was unfit for human consumption but we had no alternative but to try to eat the black bread which tasted of petrol because the burnt wheat still bore its traces and stench from the fires.

Stalin's scorched earth policy that in retreat all crops, houses and villages must be torched so that the Germans would not gain any advantages had its obvious affects also on us. It was sad that we had to bear the consequences of these acts too.

Gradually we settled down to a new pattern of life. Food was scarce and the electricity supply was cut off completely. We had only a small primus stove on which to cook and we had to be very frugal in our use of paraffin; winter and the long, dark evenings were approaching and we had no more candles.

I could tell that my mother was constantly anxious and somewhat frightened of the Germans but I found them quite interesting and many of the young ones were very attractive. No doubt this was why my mother was anxious! One young German heard that we had a piano and he and his friends would come and play and sing songs. We could not refuse them and it was circumspect to allow their simple requests without question. My mother said we should keep out of their way but I would have loved to have joined in the fun.

Mother was directed to various jobs, one of which was trying to save medicines from the broken glass and debris in a large chemist's shop in the city. Another time she was directed to work for the Germans in a small makeshift hall with other women, making white snow-overalls as camouflage for the soldiers to wear over their uniforms in the snow.

One day in November three peasant women from the village Sarabous, about seven miles away, called at our apartment. I think they were staying with neighbours. They offered food and flour in exchange for what we could offer them. Mother told me to go with them to their village and take dress material, white cotton (I wonder where she had

Had found the white cotton!) bobbins, soap and various other small items. We expected to walk all the way. It was a very cold, dark November day and the cold seemed to bite into my flesh as we trudged along. However these women hailed a German lorry and begged a lift from the Rumanian driver who, first of all, asked, 'Are you Jews?' 'Do we look like Jews?' They replied and they told him that they certainly were not. The driver didn't ask any more questions but we were very grateful to be given a lift for a few miles. We were very cold and quite hungry by the time we arrived in Sarabous. Mother had given me a small sandwich to take with me but I didn't like to eat in front of the others and waited until we reached their home.

When we arrived I stood outside their room eating the meagre sandwich but they called out, 'Come, Lydia. You must eat with us'. I hadn't seen such a feast for a very long time. We had Borsch made from cabbage, beetroot, carrots and meat stock and then chips! It was all so mouth watering. I gorged myself and every mouthful was wonderful; it was heaven. A few hours later, however, it was quite the reverse. I was in great pain and suffered very badly from having overeaten when I was already suffering from hunger and malnutrition. I did not know then, how dangerous it is to eat too much after the stomach has been accustomed to receiving very little. That was information that I had not needed to know because there seemed no likelihood of being offered more than I could safely eat.

I slept at the house house that night and the next day when I began to feel better I went from house to house to try to barter my goods. It was very cold and I must have looked a pathetic sight in my skimpy clothes and head-scarf. Success helped to warm me as I set off for home later, with eggs, butter, flour and vegetables. Two of the women came with me and we were lucky again; some Rumanian soldiers with a horse and cart gave us a lift part of the way. Back home Mother was delighted but sympathised with my unfortunate stomach trouble from gorging myself. For a while now we could enjoy a more varied diet but had to eke out the food and make it last as long as possible.

In December I met Olga, an old school friend who said that she had a job working in the hospital kitchen, performing such menial jobs as peeling potatoes and washing dishes but at least she was paid a few marks and received food in exchange for her labour. I felt a little envious so decided to go to the labour exchange and see what I could find. Mother was always

Anxious about my going out alone and one of her fears was that as I was dark haired I might be mistaken for being Jewish.

I was sent from the labour exchange to the medical school compound which had been turned into a hospital. There I was interviewed by a German lady who, I knew, happened to be Volksdeutch, that is she was born and bred in Russia although she was of German parentage. The only work she could offer me was night work. At that time I had only infrequently taken advantage of my little knowledge of the German language but when I was walking away a man called out to me, "Do you speak German?" and I replied, in German, that I most certainly did. That was it! He took me to number three building where I met a German nursing Sister who straight away gave me a job, day work, and asked me to start immediately. I was given papers to say that I was working in the hospital and my job was to sit with a wounded officer and attend to his needs. One clinical procedure I was asked to carry out was to clear a tube of pus which had gathered from an insertion into a wound. I had received no clinical training but had to use common sense. One thing I did not have to do was to give a patient a bottle. A medical orderly would be called to undertake this duty and none of the patients would submit a young girl to the embarrassment of viewing the proceedings. Apart from a few marks for wages I was to receive food, which was more acceptable.

My mother was nearly frantic when I arrived home that evening, as she had no idea where I had been or what could have happened to me. She would have been even more concerned if she had known that on my way home, which was a half-hour walk, I had been stopped by a German military policeman who called out 'Halt,' turned me around and asked to see my papers. I produced the paper given to me at the hospital, told him I was Armenian and showed my passport. He accepted this information and gruffly sent me on my way feeling very frightened for the first time. I hadn't known that Jews had been rounded up that day in town and so he was obviously on the lookout for more Jews. I had felt, at first, that this was a great adventure, then I had been afraid and finally, greatly relieved. When I was stopped for the second time on my way home I was less afraid and showed my papers with greater confidence and was once again allowed to proceed.

The next day knowing that there was food left over and thrown away after the last of the meals had been served, I took a small jug to the hospital and was allowed to take home left over food after the Russian girls had finished their meals Mother and I were more than grateful for those left-overs.

We heard one day that one of my uncles had been rounded up with other men and taken prisoner. He, at that time was 39 years old and my mother 41. He had been the last born of a family of seven and it was hinted that this last pregnancy had been unwanted and that my grandmother had tried to abort him. The result was that the boy was physically weak at birth, never robust and not, perhaps, as bright as average. He was unfit for national service or heavy physical labour and so was taken prisoner with other men who fell into a similar category, to be deported to the north.   My mother and I went to the city prison camp where we could see him beyond the barbed wire and asked if we could give him food and a blanket.   We were allowed to hand over the food but not the blanket. Perhaps the German guard thought we had secreted a weapon in the blanket!

Other men were calling out, 'Mother, please give us something to eat'. It was terrible to hear their pleas and their cries but we had nothing more to give them except our tears. It was heart rending to see the way those men were being treated. We heard soon afterwards that my uncle had died of dysentery.

Gradually we adapted to a new kind of 'normality'.   Like our neighbours, soon we had a Rumanian officer billeted with us. He slept in our apartment but I don't know where his batman slept, probably in the corridor. They were both very courteous and treated us with respect which was quite different from what we had been led to believe about the Germans.   The Rumanian officer's batman once brought us some white bread, butter and jam. Mother put on a tablecloth and made tea so that we could enjoy this rare feast in great style. I played the piano and afterwards our officer asked if I would go for a walk with him.   My mother approved and I was to take him to visit my aunt and uncle, that is my father's sister and her husband. Otto behaved very correctly and I had no need to be concerned.   I was an attractive 17 year old and he was a handsome young man and appeared to like my company.   My aunt and uncle had two German soldiers billeted in their home. It was expedient to be friendly towards them and to extend hospitality rather than be in a position where the Germans could make their own demands. Sometimes when I visited my aunt and uncle I would stay the night and have a lovely time. Aunt played the piano whilst my cousins and I danced with the Germans; it was really great fun.

All this time dreadful things were happening to the Jewish Community. We would hear of people being taken and sent, we knew not where. The Germans were constantly looking for Jews and none of them was safe. On one occasion I remember that my uncle told the German soldiers that one of my cousins was ill and she had stay in her bed. It was thought, he said, that her condition was contagious and they must not, in any circumstances, go near the bedroom. The Germans seemed perfectly satisfied with this and did nothing more than express their sympathy and hope that she would make a good recovery. Had they but known that under her bed a Jew was hiding until it was safe for him to make his escape, her health and that of the rest of the family would most certainly have been in jeopardy. Thank goodness my uncle's brave action saved at least one life.

I was learning German very fast by now and becoming more fluent. Once when our Rumanian officer took me home after an afternoon out, he said , 'Kiss me'. I was very prim and replied, 'My first kiss will be for my bridegroom and my second kiss will be for my husband'. I was so shy but he was very nice and made no further approach but soon afterwards his batman came and said they had found somewhere else to live. Mother never knew what had happened but I was sure he would soon find someone else to kiss.

Much later we had an ordinary soldier staying with us. He was from the Austrian Tyrol and was very ordinary! We received no extras but he made no advances. Sometimes Germans came to visit Kurt; sometimes Kurt and I went for walks. He would talk to me about Hitler and how life had improved for Germans since he had come to power. I was surprised to find that he knew much of Russian literature. Kurt had a wife and a child whose photographs he showed us. All these Germans and Austrians were very nice young men whose friendship we really enjoyed.

It is the Russian custom when a guest calls to offer to share food and this we always did. Although quite often some of the food had been given to us by the Germans, just occasionally, it would not feel so comfortable to offer to share what we had and perhaps we were sometimes slightly grudging in our hospitality.

Life was difficult in many ways and shortages of every commodity were to be expected. When the Germans took Uncle he had left behind a pair of his shoes and a pair of galoshes which we later used for barter, producing a whole sack of potatoes. Now we could have chips cooked in fat from the pig, and tomato ketchup, of course! We lived in this way, gleaning what we could and bartering whatever we could afford to do without. Our Russian roubles were worthless and where were we to obtain new marks? We had to walk everywhere because transport was not always available although a few trams still ran. During the winter we were very cold as there was no electricity and very little fuel. Our only light came from one oil lamp and we had no more candles. Necessity makes one bold and I used to go to the transport area at the hospital where I worked and flirt a little with the drivers who would give me some petrol for our lamp in the ketchup bottle I would take to them. And yes, we were fraternising with the Germans but we never collaborated. It was a question of expediency and survival. We took the line of least resistance but nonetheless we had to be careful.

Although we had not found the Germans to be the 'fiends and cannibals' that Stalin had described we knew that there were some Russians who would have reported those who fraternised. It was difficult in those days to consider where loyalties should lie. To some extent we were between the devil and the deep blue sea. Stalin had said in his 3rd July speech that the choice was between Soviet freedom or German slavery but how were we to judge? Life under Stalin was no picnic; could it be worse under Hitler? We could only deal with present conditions and defend ourselves; we needed to find our own way in order to survive.

At one time I fell ill with a throat infection which necessitated my staying at home for nearly three weeks. We had no antibiotics, of course, and so illnesses of that kind could become very serious and debilitating particularly when the patient was undernourished. Eventually I went back to work in a new hospital department, head injuries; this was not in the officers' quarters and other ranks were not given quite the same concessions. There were very few nurses and so my work was very much like that of an orderly except that in addition to cleaning, I had to wash the patients and feed them. One man always made me afraid as he would lunge forward when I was trying to feed him, as though he were attempting to take hold of me.

Mostly, I enjoyed the work and liked to speak German to the patients. These times were for me, if I had only known, the best parts of the war.

Changing Times

Mother and I adapted ourselves to our new circumstances, made the best of the situation, lived in present, not knowing what the future might bring but we were constantly vigilant as my headmistress had advised us to be. The Germans were short of labour in their own country as every able-bodied man of military age had been called up for national service. Women, too, were in the services and this left the Germans with the problem of a huge labour shortage which they now decided to solve by deporting women from the occupied countries to Germany. Some young women and girls had already volunteered to become 'East Workers' but I knew that it would not be long before I, too, would be on my way to Germany. The prospect did not really worry me. Again, I felt that it was, in some ways, quite exciting. My mother was less thrilled with the idea! When we discussed the matter it was decided that mother would accompany me, voluntarily, so that we need not be parted. About this time we heard that my mother's elder brother who had escaped from Crimea in 1917, taking with him whatever possessions he could, including grandmother's jewellery and other valuable items, was living in France and, in some vague but somewhat illogical way, it was thought that we might be able to contact him. With this tiny glimmer of hope at being re-united with her brother, my mother consoled herself.

A neighbour of ours had a German Army Major of about fifty years of age billeted in her house, and she had told my mother that he was a very approachable gentleman who might possibly be able to help us find suitable employment in Germany. We thought that if we could manage to make our own arrangements through various personal contacts it would be far better than being directed and not knowing where we might be sent, particularly as we had heard of the dreadful living conditions in the camps near to the factories where it was likely we might be sent. When mother met Major Schoenberg she found him to be very professional and courteous in his manner and he told her that his wife, who lived in Ludwigshafen, would be willing to employ us both as domestic servants. Arrangements would, of course, have to be made officially and the correct papers issued. We were quite happy with this arrangement and we took the philosophical notion that domestic service would probably be a lot better than most of the other jobs. On the 20th July we were ready to leave Simferopol. It had been arranged that one of the soldiers who was to accompany the group of people leaving at that time, would leave the train at Frankfurt and accompany us to Ludwigshafen.

We had cleared the house, said goodbye to everyone and departed for the station with our belongings by about 10 o'clock in the morning. Apart from our provisions for the journey we took with us as much as we could , not knowing what the future held for us. Material possessions were not a great deal of comfort but we had with us what we felt were probably the most important items: warm clothes for the winter, blankets, sheets, a few precious personal items but that was all. Cousin Senja came to help pile everything into the cart. We settled ourselves, the horse trotted off and we were on our way to a new life. It was a very emotional departure. Despite my earlier feelings of excitement, now that the time had arrived a great heaviness lay upon me. My mother tried to cheer me up but the tears flowed and I was very unhappy. The atmosphere at the station was calm. We climbed aboard the waiting train, a box train used for conveying cattle, settled ourselves in our corner with our belongings, made ourselves as comfortable as possible on the hay which was there and waited. Gradually, other girls and women came and joined us until there were about 25 of us as well as the five soldiers who were to accompany us. Gradually we began to talk with the others and wondered what the journey would be like.

There was no sign that the train was about to leave although we had been told to be at the station at a given time. We waited. The waiting became tedious and so we began to sing Russian songs in an attempt to make the time pass more quickly. It was summertime, a beautiful sunny day, we were feeling some consolation in the company of other people and we joined in the singing. Some of the girls had lovely voices and even the German soldiers showed their pleasure. Inevitably, some of the girls were very flirtatious. There were smiles and nervous laughter as the morning gently slipped by but we became a little restive in the afternoon heat. Should we eat some of our food? We knew that the journey would be long and didn't know when we might be given more food so we hesitated until we felt we could wait no longer. The future was unknown, the past was behind us, we had only the present and, so far we had not suffered in any way at the hands of the German conquerors. They had, in fact, treated us with courtesy and respect and so far we had no complaints whatsoever although we were now homeless and had no idea of what the future held for us. In comparison with the fate of so many friends and neighbours we were fortunate to be alive.

Eventually, at about five o'clock with much commotion and shouting, the train finally steamed out of the station. We rattled along, stopping quite frequently, making slow progress on a journey that was to take us ten days. Ten days in that cattle train! Ten days and ten nights which seemed interminable! We could forget about hygiene, privacy and personal appearance. Our home for those ten days and nights was a corner of a cattle truck which we shared with another thirty human beings who, too, shared our discomforts, our needs, our thoughts and concerns. We were bound by our proximity and by our condition. We travelled to Dnepropetrovsk and then west to Poland via Lvvov, then Przemysl, Krakow and then Breslau. Often the train would stop for an hour or two, sometimes longer, and we would get out to stretch our legs and, if it stopped at a station where we could find water we would be able to have a quick wash. The wash would be scarcely more than a splash as there were so many of us and we had to take our turn. We were given some food when we stopped but no more than a basic allowance. When we left the train at Breslau for a little while we felt that we had been transported into a different world. We were certainly not very clean, we were poorly dressed and obviously looking like the crushed peasants of a defeated nation (which we had become), in contrast with the fashionably dressed German ladies who wore elegant clothes, beautiful hats, smart shoes and who wore gloves and carried handbags. We were astonished to see such fashions which we thought belonged only to the very wealthy and we surely believed that we had come to a wonderful country where there were riches for all - except us! Perhaps this experience became a little unsettling and bewildering. What kind of a world was it beyond Russia? What next? It was obvious that the Germans enjoyed a very different life from the one we had known in Crimea.

We returned to the train and our next stop was Dresden, then Leipzig and finally Frankfurt where we left the train, in the charge of our German guard who was to take us to Ludwigshafen. We were almost at the end of our journey, which we then completed by taxi, to the home of the Major whom we had known in Simferopol. His wife greeted us politely, but not effusively, and we said goodbye to our German soldier escort after Frau Schoenberg had reimbursed him for the expenses of the journey from Frankfurt. The house, which obviously belonged to wealthy people, was the home of Major and Frau Schoenberg and his parents. It was very large with ample room to accommodate two more people. We had our own bathroom and, after the past ten days, were in the lap of luxury. In order to regularise our situation it was necessary for us to register, next day, at the Labour Exchange and also to submit ourselves for health checks, Frau Schoenberg having taken charge of arrangements. By the time it was my turn to see the doctor I was feeling very emotional, frightened and homesick and started to cry. The doctor spoke kindly to me and tried to put me at ease by asking where I had come from and then asked "What would you have been doing if there had not been a war?" "I would have been studying medicine," I told him, "and following in my father's footsteps." When he heard that I worked in a hospital in Simferopol and that I could speak German he told me that a Russian doctor at the hospital needed an interpreter and that he did not communicate very well with his German nurse. Dr Weiss commented on the fact that I could speak, read and write German. He smiled and asked if I would like to work in the hospital in Ludwigshafen. I couldn't believe my ears and simply whispered 'yes'. He was silent for a moment and then picked up his telephone and asked to speak to Dr. Hakobyan to whom he related my situation and it was arranged that my mother and I would meet him in the park that evening. Dr. Weiss completed the health check and noted the fact that I had eczema on my feet. My mother had been applying ointment for me but the condition, which seemed to have stemmed from insect bites - mosquito possibly, - some weeks previously, had persisted. Subsequently, I was to receive excellent treatment by the hospital consultant and the eczema cleared up completely.

That evening Dr Hakobyan arrived in the park, on his bicycle, and we sat on a park bench to discuss my employment. I had immediately recognised his name as being Armenian and my mother was pleased to be able to converse with him in her native tongue but I understood none of it; he and I spoke only in Russian. He asked if I would like to work in the hospital in Lugwigshafen if it could be arranged and I was very happy at the prospect. "There is a little difficulty over a clash of personalities there at the moment," he told me with a smile. " The fact that you can speak German and interpret could perhaps help to keep the situation more calm". Dr. Hakobyan would go ahead with the necessary arrangements and I could expect to be allowed to start work soon.

When all the documentation was in order I left, three days later, for my transfer to the hospital but because of the trouble with me feet I didn't actually start work for another few days. Mother remained with Frau Schoenberg and was treated well enough and had no complaints; she received her food ration and didn't go hungry and Frau Schoenberg gave her some clothes. Although not over familiar or friendly she was nonetheless kind and very polite which seemed to be the hallmark of most German people we encountered. We were not prisoners, of course, although we had been directed to Germany for enforced labour; we had freedom to use our off duty time as we pleased. Mother used to come to the hospital to visit me and we were able to go out together.

Ludwigshafen and Mannheim were prime industrial targets for both the Royal Air Force and the United States Air Force. We could hardly have been in a more vulnerable location. At Ludwigshafen synthetic fuel was produced and there were chemical plants and a nearby airfield. Important railroad switching systems presented vital targets at Mannheim, close to the border with France. Additionally, Mannheim was an oil production and storage site. Further targets were chemical plants, an aircraft plant, an armament factory and several bridges. It was only to be expected that we would soon experience the terror of concentrated air attacks on these twin towns. On the night of 9th/10th August the intensity of the raids reached unimaginable proportions. Everyone was very scared as we took shelter in the cellars of the Pestalozzi school. Incendiary bombs rained down as we trembled and feared for our lives. I realised afterwards that a huge Red Cross was displayed above the school and perhaps it was this that saved us.

The raids continued with some of the worst raids in early September when the two cities were completely desvastated after which time the Major's family decided to move out to the country to a safer place but not before Frau Schoenberg had deducted the cost of our journey from Frankfurt from Mother's wages and arranged to leave her, temporarily, with a neighbour three doors away. When her new employers also fled to the country mother was transferred, through the labour exchange, to the hospital where she was given work in the laundry. She and I were now together which was much better.

Our accommodation was shared with several other girls and women in a dormitory for fourteen people. We had to learn to be very circumspect, very tolerant and to accept conditions to which we had never been accustomed. We didn't like the raucous laughter, the swearing and vulgarity of some of these people but we had to live amongst them and our lives would have been a misery had we been tempted to criticise or appear judgemental in any way. We had to reconcile ourselves to the fact that some of the Russian girls were very rough, low class, uneducated people we would not have mixed with in our life in Russia. In some ways it was amusing to see them getting up at 6 o'clock, putting on their make up ready for their day's work in the kitchens. The shouting and swearing were difficult to accept but we had to get on with these girls and not allow ourselves to be snobbish. We were in no position to avoid their company and so it was better to learn to live with them. We missed our Russian friends and homesickness persisted although many people were very kind to us. Mother and I were fortunate in receiving good treatment. I had been brought up to believe that if one has the right attitude and tries to conduct oneself in the right manner life's problems become a little less daunting.

We soon learned various coping strategies and had already learned the art of expediency which helped to make life a little happier. It would not be true to say we were badly treated, suffered terrible hardships or were very unhappy but in comparison with our previous life and in comparison with the life I now know, those were, indeed, dark days. We simply made the best of things and felt it unproductive to complain. Why make ourselves unhappy by dwelling on thoughts of the past or what might have been. Other people were in similar situations, some much worse. We counted ourselves amongst the more fortunate ones.

Before we left Simferopol, I had told one of the German soldiers I had met at the hospital that I would shortly be leaving. When he asked, conversationally, if I knew where I might be going and I told him that it would be Ludwigshafen he was most interested. "Ah! My home town is Mannheim," he said. "You must visit my wife and tell her you have met me here." He gave me his home address and strict instructions to contact his wife at the first opportunity; he assured us she would be delighted to meet us. It was comforting to know that there would be at least one person we could contact on our arrival and from whom we might expect a welcome. When I eventually managed to make contact Frau Webber was every bit as welcoming as her husband, Franz, had predicted. There home was in an apartment block, nothing like the sumptuous house of the Schoenbergs, but the welcome was warm and genuine. Franz had visited us in our home in Simferopol and now Inga was kindly reciprocating that hospitality. Inga

17

was much older than me, in her early forties, and quite motherly. One day she took me, by electric train, to Heidelberg and whilst we were chatting she told me, laughingly, that Franz had written to say she should do what she could for us and suggested that she might buy a handbag for me, as I didn't have one. "Some chance," she said, "where does he think I can find a handbag? He seems to have forgotten that there's a war on!" We both laughed, as we knew that goods that were not already rationed were, by now, in very short supply. Having made contact with Inga I began to be more optimistic now that we were making friends but the friendship was short lived. The September air raids on Mannheim caused the most terrible devastation. Destruction was complete. When we went, later, to try and make contact, we saw street after street turned to rubble. Apart from the military targets huge residential areas in proximity to the factories had been razed to the ground. The tower block where the Webbers had lived had been completely gutted. We never heard from them again.

Top: UNRRA shop Lydia on the right

Bottom: UNRRA office and shop workers.
Lydia in front row with hat on.

19

Europe, 1920

Area | 1914 Boundaries | 1920 Boundaries

Top: A party of refugees at Lindau am Bodensee

Bottom: UNRRA shop staff 1946/7 Lydia in front row

Ludwigshafen Hospital

For nearly two years I enjoyed my work in the hospital. Although my work was with the doctor in the Russian wards I sometimes had to take patients to the X-ray department which was in the main building across the road. There I came in contact with the German staff, some of whom were relatively easy going and friendly but others were very stiff and formal. On the ward where I worked the staff were all Russian; there was a senior Sister, and two younger nurses as well as two male nurses. On one occasion the senior Sister came to me and said, "Oh! Lydia dear, I want you to clean the windows." Reluctantly, but obediently, I provided myself with water and cloths and started on my task. Dr Hakobyan happened to come along, and saw what I was doing and asked. "Whatever are you doing, Lydia? Who told you to clean windows?" He was most displeased and told Sister so in no uncertain terms. At first this helped to increase her resentment towards me but gradually we both learned to live with each other and I found her easier to get on with.

All the patients in the Russian wards were civilians; that is they were East Workers, like myself. One of my duties was to talk to the patients, after admission, and attempt to record their medical history and that of their family as there were, of course, no other records available. It was at this time that I began to learn that many of their parents had died of malnutrition in Ukraine in the early 1930's. Stalin's agricultural policy of collective farming, begun in 1928 had eventually failed because the peasants sabotaged the scheme by damaging machinery, destroying crops and slaughtering animals. They feared and hated the concept of collective farming, believing that more would be taken from them and that they would not even be allowed their fair share. Collectivisation, therefore, resulted in producing less, not more and it is estimated that about 5 million people died of starvation. How their offspring had survived I don't know but can only surmise that mothers would feed their children before themselves, as is the case the world over. It is hardly surprising that malnutrition resulted in a large increase in the numbers of TB and the general physical condition of these men and women had not been improved by the meagre rations they had received, first in Russia and now in Germany. Many had gastric ulcers but in addition there were other illnesses including hernias, which were very likely the result of the heavy physical labour they endured, as well as general cases of appendicitis and other surgical cases.

East Workers were required to wear a blue and white badge bearing the word 'OST' (Ost Arbeiter) meaning East Worker, on the lapel of their coats. I often went without displaying 'OST' and relied on my command of German to pass myself off as a German girl. This was a useful tactic when out with any Russian colleagues when, perhaps, we had been to the cinema or to the park and were questioned about our movements. I was, I effect, their protector. I was so much freer than if I had been in a labour camp and so lucky that because I had become fluent in German by association with native speakers it was not too difficult to affect to be German when the occasion arose and when it was expedient to do so!

I had always been keen on learning and when I found the address of a language professor who would teach me French it was arranged that I should have private lessons weekly. I was attentive and he was a good teacher; he seemed interested in me and encouraged me to learn.

One day I went to Bad Durkheim with the other girls, picking grapes, which I intended to take to his wife. When I arrived with a huge basketful I received a very warm welcome and in return for this gesture I was then allowed to play the piano once a week. Their own son was a soldier whose photograph was displayed on the piano; he was very nice looking.

My mother was pleased to encourage me with my French studies but pointed out to me that it seemed very likely that it would be the Americans and the English who would eventually be the victors and it would be a very good idea to learn a little English. When I approached my teacher he agreed to teach me and so I spent the next three months beginning to learn English.

My love of languages has stayed with me throughout my life but it most certainly made my life, and that of my mother, far better than it would have been if we had been in a labour camp, unable to communicate except in Russian. Life in the labour camps was very different from the life we led at the hospital. Cramped conditions, overcrowding and lack of privacy were a few of the contributory factors that led to a general lowering of standards and the fact that the lives of these workers were filled with sorrow, regret and uncertainty gave licence and acceptability for behaviour, for some, that would previously have been unthinkable. They had lost their homes, been taken from their motherland parted from loved ones and so the formation of relationships and increased sexual activity was possibly one form of freedom and consolation that could still be exercised. 'Live for Today' was the motto and 'don't give a thought to the possible consequences'. Moral issues were swept aside and gave way to promiscuity even amongst girls who might otherwise have remained virgins until much later.

Venereal diseases were rife and caused much suffering. Pregnancies were the usual outcome of the liaisons and were dealt with efficiently. The Germans certainly did not want to increase the number of mouths to be fed and gave authority, at an early stage of pregnancy for abortions. These were carried out in the female surgical ward and the patients returned to work as quickly as possible. Whether these operations were requested or 'advised' I can not say but I knew of only one baby that was born during my time at the hospital and that was to the wife of a Russian. Sadly, it was a breach birth and both mother and baby died.

As my mother was living in the hospital with me and I was only 18 years old she, of course, kept a strict eye on me and kept temptation as far away from me as her maternal protection could provide. There were some very attractive Czech soldiers around but they seemed as formal towards us as were the Germans. I was not unaware of them but it was probably because of my mother's influence that they appeared not to notice me! I belonged to a group of young women whose main contact with Russian male contemporaries was in a hospital ward! Love life would have to be deferred but I had no time to worry about such things just then.

**Russian Workers
Ludwigshafen
Hospital**

25

Health Problems

The greatest tank battle of the war started on 5th July 1943 and lasted for only 8 days but the number of casualties on both sides was phenomenal, Russians casualties during that time numbering a quarter of a million. Operation Citadel was Germany's last major offensive against the Russians with fierce fighting as the Germans attempted to eliminate the Kursk salient. The dreadful conditions in which these men had fought were unimaginable and their physical and mental condition was indescribable. As the Germans retreated their losses and those of the Russians were great. During the next few months there was an influx of sick and wounded Russians admitted to the hospital but before they could be admitted to a ward, male nurses had to undress the men who then had to be de-loused as part of the process of first aid before they received attention to their major injuries. The documentary evidence of their identity was retrieved and passed to me for registration and their clothing was then burnt because it was crawling with lice.

In January 1944, only a few days after a further influx of of new arrivals I became ill. On one of my visits to the cinema with some of the girls I developed a severe headache, which became so bad that I had to leave and go home to bed. The next day I was running a temperature and my condition gradually deteriorated until, on the fifth day , a rash appeared and I was delirious. The doctor took blood samples and confirmed what my mother had probably already guessed, that I was suffering from typhus. I was very ill indeed but my medication finally proved effective and my recovery began When I was feeling a little stronger Mother helped to bathe me and make me feel more comfortable and took me back to the dormitory where I normally slept. A few days later I had dreadful pains in my chest. Once again I was back to my bed and pneumonia was diagnosed. In those days when we had no penicillin or antibiotics pneumonia was a very serious illness. The illness took its course and at one stage matters became even worse when I had severe neuralgia. My mother gave me treatment with a lamp she managed to procure. One night, after the treatment, the pain was so bad that I turned to the wall and prayed, 'Oh Lord! Why are you punishing me so much?' But the treatment was already beginning to work and the next day I really did feel very much better.

It was only three weeks before the next problem, which was severe earache, so painful that I really thought I could not bear any more. The diagnosis was acute otitis media. (inflammation of the middle ear.) These illnesses lasted about three months and I began to think my problems would never end. I finally recovered sufficiently to return to work in April 1944. The origins of my illnesses can be traced back to January when I had been blissfully unaware of the risks to my own health during the course of my work. It was evident that the disease, which is carried by lice, had come my way by means of the papers, which I had handled.

The Closing Months of the War

Several of the soldiers of General Vlasov's army used to visit the nurses at the hospital where I worked. Towards the end of 1944 they would bring food and presents and there was a lighter atmosphere. There was a New Year party which I remember very well when one man played the violin. Food was brought by the soldiers and this augmented the food which some of the nurses provided, by skimping on the patients' rations and saving the food for themselves. The catholic Sisters looked after the bread which was locked up and rationed out for the patients. The Russian Sister would tell me that they were short of bread and ask me to go and ask for more; the catholic Sisters never refused but somehow the bread did not reach the patients! I found out that the bread was being taken by the Russian nurses, for barter.

The French prisoners were much freer than the rest of us and were in work camps and could go backward and forward to France and bring back various goods. They had no difficulty in finding girl friends who slept with them in return for silk underwear, nylon stockings, make up and all the luxury items which we had been denied for so long. These items, in turn, were used to barter for food and for any other commodity. I was quite disgusted when I could see what was happening and where so much of the patients' food was going. Some of the patients suffered from TB and I ordered extra milk for them but somehow that, too, disappeared and never reached the patients; only Sister knew where it went. Because she knew that I realised what was going on and that I was telling the doctors, she would try to butter me up and implicate me. To keep me quiet, she would invite me into her office and insist upon my having a glass of milk or actually bring me a glass and tell me to drink it, saying that I looked as though I needed more nourishment.

There were no real shortages for those who knew their way about the black market and for those who could barter. The French did not seem to be short of stockings and underwear and the soldiers who visited our nurses knew how to win them with such presents.

General Vlasov

General Vlasov was a Soviet war hero who had distinguished himself in the battle for Moscow. Later he was taken prisoner by the Germans and he immediately changed sides and became the highest-ranking traitor of World War II. In September 1944 after an interview with Himmler he was given official authorization to form his own Russian Liberation Army. Russian prisoners were recruited and Vlasov led them for the Germans. The soldiers who served under General Vlasov were idealists who believed that they were helping to fight against all the evils of the worst excesses of the Red Russian regime, Communism and Capitalism. There was much talk in various quarters about joining his army. It sounded very exciting, perhaps, to fight against Stalin, the Red Russian communists and Capitalism and General Vlasov was considered a hero.

In May 1945 however, when in Prague, the Czech National Army Resistance group staged an uprising and, once again Vlasov changed sides and fought against the SS garrison in the hope of delivering the city to the Americans. Vlasov's men paid the price of this adventure with their lives when the Red army entered Prague on 9th May.

In February 1945 at the Yalta Conference when the Germans were in full retreat and had, in fact, lost the war, Stalin, Churchill and Roosevelt had agreed on the division of German Territory. There was an understanding that they would exchange ech others' liberated prisoners and return them and the liberated civilians, as they were rounded up in Germany.

Accordingly, General Patton eventually sent General Vlasov back to Russia where he was hanged. It has been reported that his army of white Russian soldiers were loaded into boxcars and sent back to Russia where they were machine gunned as they got off the train.

The War in Europe ends

It was clear that the Germans had no chance of overcoming their enemies and that the war would soon be over. The air raids and bombing were frightful and the constant attacks made life sheer hell. The hospital was dealing with all the patients the could and the workload became very great. We didn't know what it was to have a proper night's sleep and our nerves were shattered. One day I found myself talking gibberish and started to shout and cry out. I had reached the stage where I simply could not take any more and became mentally ill. Lack of sleep and the stress of the constant bombing had finally caused a breakdown and I needed medical care. Some of the nurses were not very sympathetic but the wife of a caretaker could see that I was ill and took me to the laundry where my mother worked and said, 'Let's go and find your mother'. My mother took me to the big hospital where a lot of us slept at that time and I was given medical treatment with injections of phenobarbitone . After that I slept most of the time but at first with shocking nightmares. Eventually I was transferred to our dormitory on the fourth floor at the Pestalozzi school and my condition started to improve.

In the last stages of the war we slept in cellars. These bunkers had been specially built for the German patients but by now regulations regarding East Workers were not so strictly enforced and we were allowed this 'privilege'. In February the doctor gave permission for me to leave Ludwigshafen and Mother and I began our move to the south.

We start our trek South

We had saved some money as there had been very little to spend it on. There was not much one could buy and what clothing we had, had been given to us by Germans. We had no official ration allowances of any kind as we were displaced persons and dependent on others for what was given to us and so we went by train to Stuttgart and on to the Black forest area where we met Armenians who were escaping from Berlin. There were many, many refugees and much confusion. We traveled together with some people to Rottweill where the local authorities allowed us to sleep in school halls. We walked around the town and I found a job in a hospital, having good references from Ludwigshafen and we found lodgings with a German family who knew that the French were advancing and it would be better to have two women occupying their rooms instead of having to accommodate French soldiers.

The war ended in May 1945 but for us it was simply a time of confusion, waiting and wondering what to do next. The war in Europe might be over but our destiny had yet to be decided. We were not sure where to go. French troops were now in occupation and some of their soldiers were Moroccan and Algerian. These bearded, turbaned men looked strange to us and had a frightening appearance.

We were very concerned in case we were to be repatriated with refugees from some of the camps. This uncertainty and anxiety persisted until July when, together with an Armenian and his Russian wife we decided to go to Lindau am Bodensee, Lake Constance in Germany. We had heard that General Lampe a white Russian emigre was giving certificates to refugees in order to help establish an identity. The last thing we wanted was to be sent back to Russia and my mother astonished me by stating that we were Persian. With a suitable identity we might be granted entry to an hospitable country. We had grand ideas of perhaps going to the U S A, anywhere except Germany or Russia. We started our journey and walked for five days, a distance of about 125 Km. To Lindau am Bodensee, sleeping wherever we could find a night's lodging and begging food from any likely source. The Armenian, who could speak French, would often beg from the soldiers on our behalf asking, " are there any left-overs?" Sometimes the French soldiers would give us some of their food and we found most people were kind and helped us when they could. One night we slept in a barn on hay like so many other refugees. After five days we eventually arrived in Lindau and were able to register with General Lampe.

Godmother to baby Irena
In Lindau 1946

Lindau

When we arrived in Lindau I saw a young girl who was buying sweets at a kiosk. She spoke to me and suggested I should go along with her as she could find good lodgings for us. We went along with her and saw the room with four beds and were very pleased. Soon the girl came back into the room and said I should go with her to meet some French soldiers and have some drinks and food. There were a few people there who seemed very pleasant and after a while they all left the room except for one man who was very nice to me. He offered me an apartment for all four of us and said there would be no shortages of anything, plenty of food and then - the penny dropped! The girl at the kiosk had been procuring on his behalf. He said his previous girlfriend was 'no good' and I told him I was 'no good' either and was emphatic in my refusal. I felt a little shaken and somewhat afraid of what might happen next but didn't say anything to my mother. I probably, naively, thought that if I didn't think about it everything would be all right. At 5 am next morning I should not have been surprised when there was banging and thumping on our door and we were all told to GET OUT and were unceremoniously ejected.

We walked another 10 KM. To Schlachters, a large village where we went to the Burgomaster and asked for help. He found us a large room with beds for all and our work was to pick up the windfall apples from the ground and then start picking them from the trees. It was sometime after this that mother and the Russian woman fell out following some foolish quarrel originating over some minor criticism of me, which my mother refused to accept. As neither was willing to give way we parted company and moved on to another farm and met more refugees. We heard of other Armenian refugees in a nearby village and went one day, to meet them. We became very friendly with a couple and their son, Nicholas, about my own age. Nicholas and I soon became good friends. I went for rides with him on his motor bike, he took me to the village dances where we had some really good times and as we grew more fond of each other we would go for walks in the woods to be alone together.

Nicholas was the only child of an adoring and adored mother. I had to be satisfied with being second in his affection. However, we were happy together and he was good to me. He knew that I would dearly have liked to own a bicycle and so he built one for me from parts that he was able to acquire from various sources. The farmer paid us in apples, quite literally the fruits of our labour. He also produced apple by-products such as schnapps which formed another medium of currency. Two litres of schnapps were bartered for tyres and handlebars. What other forms of barter took place I can't remember but Nicholas managed to acquire all the necessary parts. I had great times with that bicycle. Both Nicholas and my mother had such patience teaching me to ride and I felt so thrilled when I could wobble along without their help.

Unlike today's modern bikes the braking system was rather like that of a ship; that is, in order to slow down one had to back pedal, and if one wanted to stop it was necessary to be very skilful in back pedalling! I had not fully mastered the art and as I was speeding down a steep hill one day and wished to make a left hand turn at the bottom of the hill, I made an unsuccessful attempt to back pedal and I shot over the handlebars, landing in a heap with the bicycle somewhere in the vicinity, both of us very much the worse for wear. I suffered from two broken arms and a badly lacerated face. My bicycle suffered from broken spokes and twisted wheels. A passerby took me to Lindau hospital for emergency treatment to my broken bones and sore face. I looked a sorry sight when my mother, who had been frantic with worry about my late homecoming, finally saw me. All night I was in agony and needed more help than my poor mother could provide.

Next day a local farmer brought out his tractor and took me back to Lindau where I was admitted to the hospital and remained there for about a week. During this time I was disappointed that Nicholas didn't visit me, even once. He was not proving to be the knight in shining armour I had thought him to be but I had to forgive him when I learned that it was my bicycle that was receiving all his attention and he hoped to have it back on the road for me as soon as I was fit to ride it again.

When I came out of hospital my mother was very ill with pneumonia and it was her turn to be hospitalised. Nicholas' parents were most kind and insisted that I should go and stay with them until I was able to look after myself. When my mother was discharged from hospital she was taken to the local cottage hospital for convalescing as there had been concerns regarding the possibility that she might be suffering from Tuberculosis. Whilst I was recovering and my bones were mending, Nicholas completed the repairs to my bicycle and in due course we were able to resume our rides together and our walks in the woods. It was inevitable that Nicholas and I should become lovers as our long and close relationship developed. We were so happy together and so much in love that nothing else seemed to matter. The war was over and we would, eventually, be able to make a future together, we thought. Like all lovers our heads were in the clouds when the reality was that we had nothing, we were both refugees, our future was uncertain; in fact we were both too much in love to face reality.

However, the time came when I had to face it myself. When I discovered I was pregnant I was absolutely devastated and soon began to realise the dreadful implications of my predicament. I had no rosy future; I had glaring reality. Reality was the word that kept repeating itself. I was frightened and in despair. The truth was that I would now always be a refugee, as no country would accept children. My mother would also have to remain a refugee, as I knew she would not leave me. Tears were to no avail; desperate action was called for. My mother was most unhappy but very practical despite her abhorrence of what she knew we must do. Fortunately she was able to arrange for me to make an appointment to see a doctor who resolved the situation for us and then she made it perfectly clear that my association with Nicholas must end immediately if we were to stand a chance of being accepted in any country other than Germany or Russia. The doctor was discreet and life was quickly restored to its previous state. His payment, incidentally, was in cigarettes as the barter system and black market persisted for as long as we were still in Germany.

The months that followed were some of the unhappiest times of my life. Not only did I suffer from the guilt I felt for my actions but also my heart was breaking because I had loved Nicholas. Mother was kind and didn't refer to the matter again. We lived in the farmer's house and worked there until October. At the end of the season we received our wages. Our payment, as I mentioned, was in apples so it was necessary for us to sell them if we wanted to change them for more useful currency. We had a little money so we set off for Munich, bought our return tickets and boarded the train with our box of apples.

In Munich we were told, there were shortages of every kind and we would soon be able to convert the apples into hard cash. It wasn't long before we had sold all except those we had left in a safe deposit at the station. At 5 marks for each apple we thought we would soon be quite wealthy! We were feeling very pleased with ourselves and were just about to return to the station to collect them when I felt a hand on my shoulder and turned abruptly to face an un-uniformed German police officer who showed me his ID; we had, of course, been engaged in criminal activity, selling on the black market. I lost no time in grabbing the moneybag from my mother, then squirmed and pushed away the policeman and ran as fast as I could. When I caught my breath I could not see either the policeman or my mother and I began to be quite afraid. The situation filled me with guilt as well as fear. From behind a pillar I tried to keep watch for some time but they both seemed to have disappeared. My conscience prompted me to go searching for my mother whom I had abandoned and I went first to the German police who couldn't help me at all and then I made further enquiries at the American headquarters but again , to no avail. By now it would have been about 4 p.m. and I was most agitated and tearful and decided to return to the camp to see if Mother had returned. I met a lady who saw how upset I was and after hearing the sad tale of the lost mother suggested that I should go back with her to the railway station in Munich to see whether she was there. Imagine my relief and joy when I found her waiting patiently for me without any reproaches at all as we were only too happy to be reunited. We were able to express our gratitude to this lady by giving her the apples from the safe deposit box.

The question of obtaining official identity papers was a major concern for us and we decided to go, one day, to Ravensbruch to see the Swiss Consulate for this purpose. We needed to establish the fact that we were not from USSR and explained that all our papers were lost and we needed documentation in order to apply for entry to a country that might take us. We knew, of course, that according to international agreement prisoners and workers were to be sent back to their own countries and we very afraid that we would be sent back to Russia. My mother spoke first and said we were Armenians from Persia (Iran) and asked whether they would please send to Persia for our birth certificates. It was agreed that this would be done and in the meanwhile we were given our official documents, printed on embossed paper, written in French, giving us authority to be treated as displaced persons with a view to being accepted in the UK. We were very happy to receive such documentation as it was extremely likely when it was shown to a German burgomaster who couldn't speak French, that he would only see the word IRAN and that was all that mattered. If a Russian officer then asked him if there were any displaced Russian people he could say No. Our birth certificates were never found, of course, and even after our arrival in England we were very much afraid to tell the truth about our nationality. Russians were hardly 'flavour of the month' but Romanians, Iranians, Polish and others were welcome in UK.

Much later, in 1948, I was very scared when I received a letter saying that I must go for an interview to the Home Office in London. There I was questioned for some considerable time as there seemed to have been some irregularity regarding my papers. I was asked to say exactly where I was born, the name of the street and the town, questions which I could not answer without telling more lies. When I could no longer conceal the truth I broke down and blurted out, 'Yes, Yes, I am Russian but my mother and I would rather be in the Thames than go back there'. My interrogator was silent for a moment but eventually, seeming satisfied that we were no risk to national security, he spoke quietly and calmly to me and I was sent on my way, much relieved that we were not about to be deported to Russia.

The New Year party in 1946
Lydia is on extreme right

New Beginnings and the prospect of leaving Germany

In the winter of 1945/6 UNRRA (United Nations Relief and Rehabilitation Administration) set up an office in Lindau where displaced persons could register and where they were given Red Cross food parcels. In the spring of '46 I was offered work in the UNRRA shop which received Red Cross parcels. My job was to open the parcels and make new ones which would be suitable for men, women and children. We received a small ration each week and I was asked to look after the children's department - clothing and toys, not food. After several months I was transferred to do clerical work in their office until September 1947.

In August an English officer arrived in Lindau to organise an important meeting for displaced persons. He had come to offer work, mainly for women and girls. We were told about life in England, the climate, the people and what jobs were available. Girls and women between the ages of 18 and 49 were wanted to work in various occupations. Mother, at that time was just 49 and she was very keen for us to take a chance to go to England rather than wait for a different opportunity and perhaps be over the age limit. We registered and were given ID cards and ration books. During the next couple of weeks we packed what we wanted to keep and sold anything else for as much as we could get.

At the end of September we went by train from Lindau To north Germany to a big camp where we were submitted to both medical and political checks. There we spent two weeks before being moved on again, by train, to the Hook of Holland. When the ship sailed from the Hook we were at last on our way to another new life. During the crossing as we had no English money we were each given One Pound (sterling) which seemed a vast amount of money when one considers that five pound, at that time, would have been a reasonable weekly wage for a man. Mother did not enjoy the sea crossing to Harwich and was sick most of the time. It is difficult to remember my mixed emotions on arrival in the UK. It was the beginning of a great adventure but there was also fear of the unknown especially as neither of us spoke English but we had endured so much for so long that we could only live from day to day and try to adapt. We were neither of us, in rude good health but our spirits were strong and we were ready to start a new phase in our lives.

In Harwich we were placed in a reception centre to be checked once again and then on to Newmarket by coach to a camp at West Wratting. There we stayed for about 2 - 3 weeks whilst we considered our limited options and made choices. The options including working in the cotton industry in the north of England but Mother and I wanted to be together and to be near to London and were finally sent to Hertford.

We make our home in England

Mother and I lodged in a house in Cromwell Road, Hertford. Mother spoke not one word of English, only Russian. I spoke fluent German, a little French and a little English. We were found work in the Model Laundry, not the kind of work a professional woman and her daughter would have done had it not been for the war but we were glad to be alive, to have arrived in England, have a little money of our own and our new found independence. We lodged with a lady who, like many other people locally, had taken displaced persons from Poland as lodgers. Life was difficult for us without adequate means of communication. Life is sterile without books and access to knowledge. As the first and most important, step to becoming rehabilitated I wanted desperately to master the language.

One morning as I was leaving the house a young boy approached me and asked, very courteously, "Excuse me, do you speak Polish?" I told him, haltingly, that I was Russian, couldn't speak Polish and asked him who wanted to know. "My teacher," he replied, "I told her there were two ladies in our road I thought were Polish and she asked me to find out 'cos she's got a Polish worker in her house". "I need someone to teach me English," I told him, and asked him to tell his teacher. It was not long after that, that Alice contacted me and started to teach me. I earned enough at the laundry to be able to pay for my lodgings and, having been used to the hardships of a life in wartime Germany our wants were few and there was enough to pay Alice the small sum she asked for tuition.

I was a good student, having an aptitude for languages, and although having lacked further education my basic education to the age of fifteen had been good. It had been my intention to follow in my father's footsteps and become a doctor but the world had turned upside down and survival was the only thing to care about. Alice soon recognised my potential and, like all good teachers who discover a promising pupil, was determined to see that my talents were not wasted.

"What do you really want to do with your life, Lydia? What had been your ambitions before the war?" I told her I wanted to follow a career in medicine, how my father had died, the war had come, then the Germans had sent us to work in Germany and now it was too late to do anything except work in a laundry. We both laughed at the absurdity of the situation and the nonsense, she said, of tolerating the present conditions. "You don't have to work in a laundry, you know. You have the ability to do many things you are only 22 years old. You must take charge of your life and not let adverse circumstances rule you". Alice encouraged me to reach the necessary standard in my English and to apply for nursing training.

Alice was ten years older than me, my role model, my heroine and my friend. I would go to her house for my lessons and feel that she was the very model of an English lady. She was happily married and, to me, was the epitome of Englishness. I recall that Mum and I were out visiting the Tower of London one day when we saw Alice with a gentleman, not her husband, Alice introduced us and we chatted for a little while. Before my next lesson Alice wrote to me and asked me not to mention the meeting to her husband. The sharing of Alice's secret seemed to make us closer friends and we remained so until after her death a few years ago. Although my ambition was to become a fully qualified nurse I came across an advertisement which attracted my attention because of my knowledge of foreign languages. Telephone operators were being recruited for handling inter-continental calls and I thought this might be a good opportunity for me. However, my application did not get very far as I was under five feet in height and the minimum height had to be the full sixty inches!

Undeterred, I returned to my earlier ambitions, did well in my exams, became a State Registered Nurse, married an Englishman whom I adored and Mum came to live with us and was always happy to help with our small family. I was in my seventh heaven and had so much to thank Alice for. Yes, I had taken charge of my life.

Our landlady said she needed our room for her son and she wanted us to leave so I went to Alice and told her of our difficulty. Alice was tall and had quite an imposing manner. She took me to the police and asked for help for me. The police directed us to the Christian Alliance Women and Girls Hostel. Alice went with me where I was interviewed, Alice acting as interpreter on my behalf. I was asked to return the next day with my mother so that we could both be interview together. Mother wore her best coat and hat and set out to impress. The house seemed very comfortable and we were delighted when we were given a room. There were about twelve women and girls there, two of whom were Welsh and two Scottish. I remember there was a big cat that would sit contentedly by the fire. We, too, were very contented there: we were like one big happy family. We enjoyed very good food, which was cooked for us and this was a really lovely home. There was only one bathroom for all of us and so we had our roster for the week but this was not unusual in 1948 and I am sure we were all perfectly clean. As Florence Nightingale said 'one pint of water is all that is necessary to be clean'.

Downstairs in the sitting room there was a piano and I remember what a joy it was to go down there and play. The first tune I played, and sang was 'I'll be your sweetheart, if you will be mine; all my life I'll be your valentine'. Whilst I was there Alice continued teaching me English and gave me constant encouragement to work hard to reach my goal. I was able to change my job and work as an auxiliary nurse at theHertford Hospital. I made application to various London teaching hospitals to enrol on their nursing courses but because I hadn't thecorrect educational qualifications I was refused entry. However, I applied to the Prince of Wales General Hospital in Tottenham where after taking their own entrance examination I passed and was accepted for training. There were more hard times to follow. Although on the one hand we had our freedom and were beginning to make plans for the future, we had no control over such things as ill health. Mother, sadly, became mentally ill and required psychiatric treatment at Claybury Hospital. Trying to care for her and to carry on with my work and study for exams in order to qualify as a State Registered Nurse was very hard indeed but I coped.

It was during this time that I met Dennis who encouraged me and showed me so much kindness. After receiving my State registration and marrying Dennis we moved into our first home together with my mother, whose mental health had improved considerably. No matter what lay ahead, what difficulties the future might bring, at that time I believed I was the luckiest woman alive and so grateful to have met such a wonderful man with whom to share my life. My mother's health gave us problems from time to time with intermittent spells of hospitalisation but there were many happy times when she was able to be a loving mother and grand-mother, loved and cared for by Dennis and me until her death in 1979. Our one child, Anne, brought us great joy and is a great comfort to me in my twilight years. In 2002 we travelled together with my grand-daughter, Rifka, to Crimea to see , once more, the country where I was born. In the sixty years that have passed since I left Simferopol it has changed so much. Pushkin Street was more or less as I had remembered it, the library where father had sometimes worked was still the same but I felt vaguely disappointed and realised that what was missing could never be replaced. The people I had known and loved had all gone with the passing of time, leaving me only waves of nostalgia. Whatever I felt on my return to Russia, my over-riding emotion was the satisfaction of

having shown my daughter and grandchild where it had all started, where their Armenian ancestors had come from. It had been necessary to go back to close the circle. That part of my life has been over for many years; those chapters closed. My story is recounted to fill the gaps of those years in between.

Lydia in Hertford 1948

Lydia, Dennis and Anne on Holiday in Bournemouth 1957